U.S. CHEMICAL SAFETY AND HAZARD INVESTIGATION BOARD

I0489297

INVESTIGATION REPORT

CATASTROPHIC VESSEL FAILURE

(1 Killed, Community Evacuation, and Shelter-in-Place)

D. D. WILLIAMSON & CO., INC.
LOUISVILLE, KENTUCKY
APRIL 11, 2003

KEY ISSUES
OVERPRESSURE PROTECTION
HAZARD EVALUATION SYSTEMS
LAYERS OF PROTECTION
OPERATING PROCEDURES AND TRAINING

REPORT NO. 2003-11-I-KY
MARCH 2004

Abstract

This investigation report examines a vessel explosion that occurred on April 11, 2003, at D. D. Williamson & Co., Inc., in Louisville, Kentucky. The explosion caused a massive release of aqua ammonia. Twenty-six residents were evacuated, and 1,500 people were sheltered in place. This report identifies the root and contributing causes of the incident and makes recommendations on overpressure protection, hazard evaluation systems, layers of protection, and operating procedures and training.

The U.S. Chemical Safety and Hazard Investigation Board (CSB) is an independent Federal agency whose mission is to ensure the safety of workers, the public, and the environment by investigating and preventing chemical incidents. CSB is a scientific investigative organization; it is not an enforcement or regulatory body. Established by the Clean Air Act Amendments of 1990, CSB is responsible for determining the root and contributing causes of accidents, issuing safety recommendations, studying chemical safety issues, and evaluating the effectiveness of other government agencies involved in chemical safety.

No part of the conclusions, findings, or recommendations of CSB relating to any chemical incident may be admitted as evidence or used in any action or suit for damages arising out of any matter mentioned in an investigation report (see 42 U.S.C. § 7412 [r][6][G]). CSB makes public its actions and decisions through investigation reports, summary reports, safety bulletins, safety recommendations, case studies, incident digests, special technical publications, and statistical reviews. More information about CSB may be found at www.csb.gov.

Salus Populi Est Lex Suprema
People's Safety is the Highest Law

Information about available publications may be obtained by contacting:

U.S. Chemical Safety and Hazard Investigation Board
2175 K Street NW, Suite 400
Washington, DC 20037-1848
(202) 261-7600

CSB publications may be purchased from:

National Technical Information Service
5285 Port Royal Road
Springfield, VA 22161-0002
(800) 553-NTIS or
(703) 487-4600
Email: info@ntis.fedworld.gov

For international orders, see:
www.ntis.gov/support/cooperat.htm.

For this report, refer to NTIS number PB2004-103035.

Contents

Figures

Figures

Acronyms and Abbreviations

AIChE	American Institute of Chemical Engineers
ASME	American Society of Mechanical Engineers
ATF	Bureau of Alcohol, Tobacco, Firearms and Explosives
CCPS	Center for Chemical Process Safety
CFR	Code of Federal Regulations
cp	Centipoise
CSB	U.S. Chemical Safety and Hazard Investigation Board
cGMP	Current Good Manufacturing Practice (FDA)
DDW	D. D. Williamson & Co., Inc.
EMA	Emergency Management Agency
EPA	U.S. Environmental Protection Agency
°F	Degrees Fahrenheit
FDA	U.S. Food and Drug Administration
IDLH	Immediately dangerous to life and health
KAR	Kentucky Administrative Regulations
NSC	National Safety Council
NIOSH	National Institute for Occupational Safety and Health
OSHA	Occupational Safety and Health Administration
PEL	Permissible exposure limit
ppm	Parts per million
psi	Pounds per square inch
psig	Pounds per square inch gage
PSM	Process Safety Management (OSHA)
RIMS	Risk and Insurance Management Society, Inc.
RMP	Risk Management Program (EPA)

Executive Summary

An April 11, 2003, vessel explosion at the D. D. Williamson & Co., Inc. (DDW), plant in Louisville, Kentucky, killed one operator. The explosion damaged the western end of the facility and released 26,000 pounds of aqua ammonia (29.4 percent ammonia solution in water), forcing the evacuation of as many as 26 residents and requiring 1,500 people to shelter-in-place.

DDW used the vessel in the manufacture of food-grade caramel coloring. It functioned as a feed tank for a spray dryer that produced powdered colorants. The feed tank, which was heated with steam and pressurized with air, was operated manually. To ensure that the filling, heating, and material transfer processes stayed within operating limits, operators relied on their experience and on readouts from local temperature and pressure indicators.

The feed tank most likely failed as a result of overheating the caramel color liquid, which generated excessive pressure.

In investigating this incident, the U.S. Chemical Safety and Hazard Investigation Board (CSB) determined the following causes:

- DDW did not have effective programs in place to determine if equipment and processes met basic process and plant engineering requirements. The tank that failed had no relief device for overpressure protection, nor did it have basic process control or alarm instrumentation to prevent process upsets. DDW had no program for evaluating vessel fitness for service and no management system for evaluating the effect of equipment changes on safety.

- DDW did not have adequate hazard analysis systems to identify feed tank hazards, nor did it effectively use contractors and consultants to evaluate and respond to associated risks.

- DDW did not have adequate operating procedures or adequate training programs to ensure that operators were aware of the risks of allowing the spray dryer feed tanks to overheat and knew how to respond appropriately.

An April 11, 2003, vessel explosion at the D. D. Williamson & Co., Inc., plant in Louisville, Kentucky, killed one operator.

The feed tank most likely failed as a result of overheating the caramel color liquid, which generated excessive pressure.

The tank . . . had no relief device for overpressure protection, nor did it have basic process control or alarm instrumentation to prevent process upsets.

CSB makes substantive recommendations to DDW regarding hazard evaluation programs and plant operations. Furthermore, CSB recommends that the Commonwealth of Kentucky communicate regulatory requirements regarding used vessels to businesses and other entities in the State and that the Mechanical Contractors Association of Kentucky communicate the same to its members. CSB also recommends that the Risk and Insurance Management Society and the National Board of Boiler and Pressure Vessel Inspectors share the information in this investigation report with their members.

1.0 Introduction

1.1 Background

At approximately 2:10 am on Friday, April 11, 2003, a vessel at the D. D. Williamson & Co., Inc. (DDW), plant in Louisville, Kentucky, exploded. One operator was killed; the other four men working at the plant at the time of the incident were not injured. Twenty-six thousand pounds of aqua ammonia (29.4 percent ammonia in water solution) was released; 26 residents were evacuated and 1,500 were sheltered-in place. The explosion caused extensive damage to the western end of the facility.

Because of the serious nature of this incident—the worker fatality, neighborhood evacuation, and extent of damage—the U.S. Chemical Safety and Hazard Investigation Board (CSB) launched an investigation to determine the root and contributing causes and to issue recommendations to help prevent similar occurrences.

1.2 Investigative Process

CSB investigators arrived at the plant on the morning of April 12. The Louisville Fire Department controlled the accident scene. Also onsite were the Louisville Police Department; Louisville/Jefferson County Emergency Management Agency (EMA); Division of Occupational Safety and Health Compliance, Kentucky Labor Cabinet (now a part of the Environment and Public Protection Cabinet); and Bureau of Alcohol, Tobacco, Firearms and Explosives (ATF).

In conducting its independent investigation, CSB examined physical evidence, interviewed DDW management and hourly employees, and reviewed relevant documents with the full cooperation of DDW. In addition to the organizations named above, CSB also had extensive discussions with the Boiler Inspection Section of the Kentucky Division of Fire Prevention, Office of State Fire Marshal, regarding the State's regulatory apparatus and practices for pressure vessels.

1.3 Plant Operations

DDW is the world's largest producer of caramel coloring for food products, including cola drinks, sauces, and seasonings. The DDW plant in Louisville—the company's largest site—employs approximately 45 people and has been in operation since 1948. The plant is located in a mixed industrial and residential neighborhood, 1.5 miles east of downtown Louisville. The Kentucky School for the Blind is located several blocks north of the plant. DDW corporate offices are located within walking distance of the plant. Other DDW plants are located in South America, Europe, Africa, and Asia.

At the time of the incident, the following employees handled technical issues at the DDW Louisville facility:

- A president with 11 years of experience at DDW.

- A plant manager with 8.5 years of experience.

- A technical coordinator, who was completing a Masters degree in chemical engineering and had been employed at DDW for 3 years.

An assistant plant manager with over 40 years of operating and safety experience was in the process of retiring. The experience of operators in the spray dryer area ranged from 3 months to 22 years.

DDW produces caramel color by two methods (Kamuf, Nixon, and Parker, 2000):

- Maillard reaction, in which liquid sugars (glucose, fructose, etc.) are heated and reacted with either ammonia or ammonium bisulfite to form brown pigments.

- Caramelization reaction, which is carried out in the absence of nitrogen compounds. The reactions are run at approximately 300 degrees Fahrenheit (°F).

DDW distributes approximately 85 percent of its product in liquid form. The remaining 15 percent is converted from liquid to powder in a spray dryer. The plant runs 24 hours/day, 7 days/week; operators work 12-hour shifts.

The April 11 incident occurred in the spray dryer area at the west end of the plant (Figure 1). The spray dryer was located 6 feet north of feed tank #2 (Section 1.5), the tank that exploded.

Corrugated aluminum walls enclosed the spray dryer area, and a concrete block wall to the east separated it from other processing areas of the facility. The aqua ammonia storage tank was one of four tanks located just outside and to the west of the spray dryer area; of the other three tanks, one was empty, one was a 12,000-gallon horizontal tank of 50 percent caustic soda, and one was a 20,000-gallon vertical tank of ammonium bisulfite.

The April 11 incident occurred in the spray dryer area at the west end of the plant.

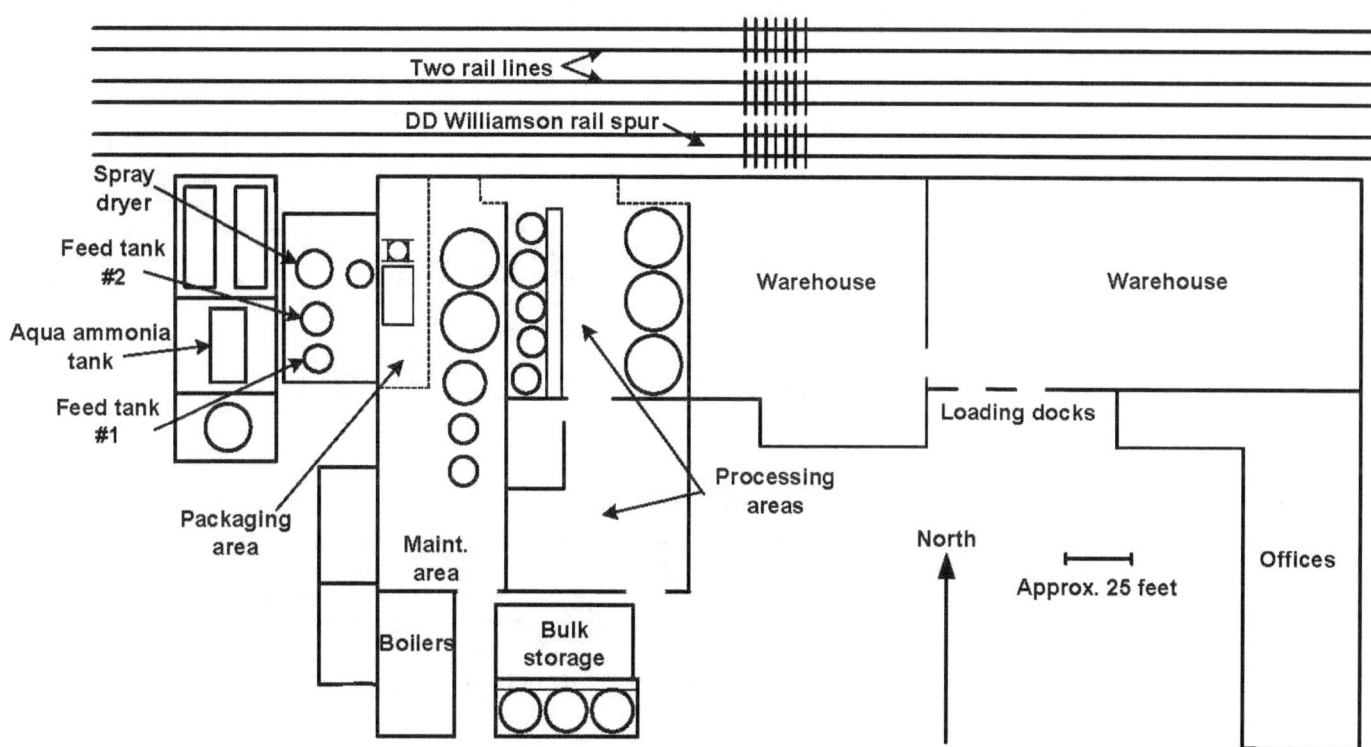

Figure 1. DDW plant layout.

1.4 Spray Dryer System Operation

One 1,800-gallon tank (feed tank #1) and one 2,200-gallon tank (feed tank #2) fed the DDW spray dryer (Figure 2). These stainless-steel pressure vessels were equipped with internal stainless-steel coils for heating with steam or cooling with water and with agitators for mixing.

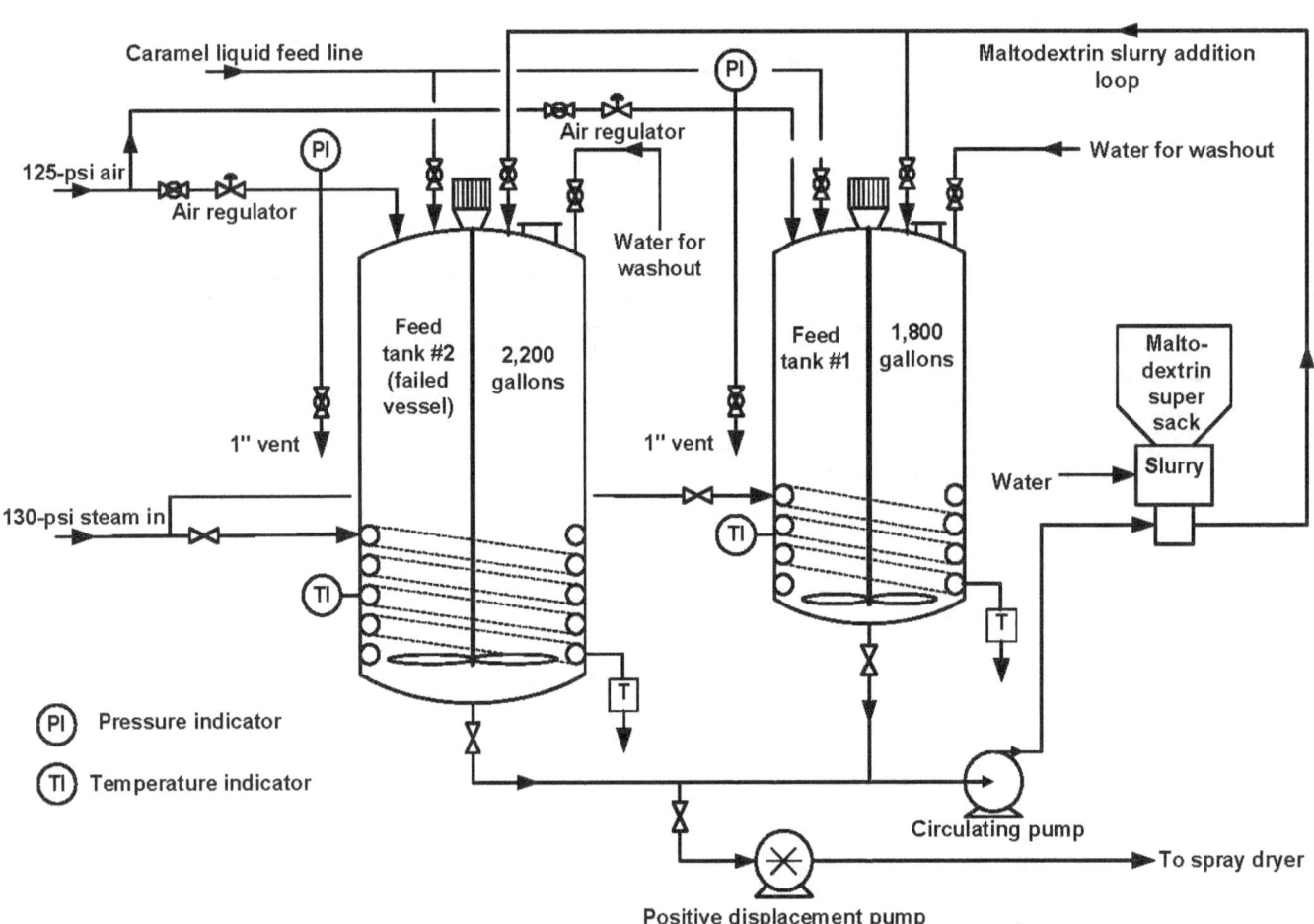

Figure 2. Feed tank flow schematic.

To prepare the spray dryer feed, the tank was partially filled with caramel color liquid and maltodextrin, a carrying agent used to improve spray dryer performance.[1] The maltodextrin, accounting for 10 percent of the total feed mixture, was slurried with water and added to the caramel color liquid through an eduction loop. The product being prepared at the time of the incident had a very high viscosity (2,200 centipoise [cp]); it was the highest viscosity caramel used for spray dryer feed at DDW.[2] The mixture was heated to 160°F using steam on the feed tank coils. These measures lowered the viscosity and improved the ability to pump the mixture to the spray dryer and force it through the dryer nozzles.

To assist in the transfer of material from the feed tank to the spray dryer feed pump, the tank was pressurized with air at approximately 22 pounds per square inch (psi) using the compressed air system. Self-contained pressure regulators modulated the air pressure to each feed tank from the plant header pressure of 125 pounds per square inch-gage (psig) to 20 to 25 psig. Each feed tank had a 1-inch vent line with valve tied into the air line. It was necessary to close the vent valve to add pressure to the feed tank. When the feed tank was emptied, the vent line was opened to allow pressure to bleed off.

A positive displacement feed pump raised the pressure of the mixture to more than 4,000 psi—to force the liquid through the atomizer nozzles at the top of the spray dryer and create the desired particle size. The material fell 25 feet through the spray dryer chamber, while air heated to 600°F flowed up. By the time the material reached the bottom of the chamber, it was dried to powder.

On each shift, two operators worked in the spray dryer area of the plant. In addition to producing the spray-dried product detailed above, the operators filled and labeled product containers (typically plastic bags placed inside cardboard boxes), and moved them to warehouse areas using forklift trucks.

The product being prepared at the time of the incident had a very high viscosity (2,200 centipoise); it was the highest viscosity caramel used for spray dryer feed at DDW.

To assist in the transfer of material from the feed tank to the spray dryer feed pump, the tank was pressurized with air at approximately 22 psi . . .

A positive displacement feed pump raised the pressure of the mixture to more than 4,000 psi— to force the liquid through the atomizer nozzles at the top of the spray dryer and create the desired particle size.

In addition to producing the spray-dried product . . . the operators filled and labeled product containers . . .

[1]Maltodextrin is a dried powder carbohydrate produced from corn starch.
[2]By comparison, the viscosity of honey is approximately 10,000 cp.

1.5 Feed Tanks

Drawings show that tank #2 was built with a maximum working pressure of 40 psi . . . There is no evidence that the tanks were designed, fabricated, or tested in accordance with the ASME Boiler and Pressure Vessel Code . . .

Before their arrival in Louisville, both tanks [feed tanks #1 and #2] had been used in the manufacture of ammonium bisulfite, a raw material for caramel color.

CSB also learned that tank #2 had been deformed on two occasions due to the misapplication of vacuum, and was then refitted and returned to service.

Feed tank #2—the 2,200-gallon vessel that failed—was 7.5 feet in diameter and 8 feet tall. It was built in 1977. Feed tank #1— 6 feet in diameter and also 8 feet tall—was built in 1965. Eastern Tank Fabricators, Inc., of New York, built both tanks, which were constructed of 316 stainless steel. The tank insulation was protected from damage by aluminum sheeting, which was held in place by aluminum retaining bands.

Drawings show that tank #2 was built with a maximum working pressure of 40 psi; the maximum working pressure of tank #1 was 25 psi. Neither tank was rated for vacuum service. There is no evidence that the tanks were designed, fabricated, or tested in accordance with the American Society of Mechanical Engineers (ASME) Boiler and Pressure Vessel Code, Section VIII, the standard for pressure vessels in the United States.

Although detailed records were not available, the following chronological history of the tanks was reconstructed through employee interviews:

- Tank #1 was originally put into service in Dallas, Texas, and was moved to Louisville in 1982 when the Dallas facility was closed.

- Tank #2 was originally used at a DDW plant in Long Island City, New York. In 1981, it was moved to another DDW plant, in Piscataway, New Jersey; and in 1989, it was moved to Louisville for use in the new spray drying process.

Before their arrival in Louisville, both tanks had been used in the manufacture of ammonium bisulfite, a raw material for caramel color. The tanks were operated at atmospheric pressure and were equipped with pressure relief devices at the time.

CSB also learned that tank #2 had been deformed on two occasions due to the misapplication of vacuum, and was then refitted and returned to service. Details of these repairs were not available; however, one employee recalled that the tank welds were not x-rayed to ensure tank integrity.

DDW did not notify the Commonwealth of Kentucky that it was bringing the two tanks into the State, as required by Kentucky boiler and pressure vessel regulations, nor did DDW register the tanks with the State.

As installed in Louisville, the feed tanks had no safety valves or rupture disks. Each tank was equipped with a 1-inch vent line, terminating in a manual valve, which operators used to relieve pressure (Section 1.4). The tanks were placed on weigh cells to measure batch quantities; there was no other automatic instrumentation. A temperature gauge located midway up the tank shell and a pressure gauge on the air feed manifold were the only instruments associated with the tanks.

As installed in Louisville, the feed tanks had no safety valves or rupture disks. Each tank was equipped with a 1-inch vent line, terminating in a manual valve, which operators used to relieve pressure.

A temperature gauge located midway up the tank shell and a pressure gauge on the air feed manifold were the only instruments associated with the tanks.

On the day shift on April 10, 2003, the spray dryer operators had completed processing one dried product and had begun preparing the system for the next product. This task involved cleaning out the spray dryer and the two feed tanks with hot water. The operators then filled feed tank #1, the smaller of the two tanks, with caramel color liquid and the maltodextrin carrying agent, and heated the tank to 160°F. They also cleaned and emptied feed tank #2 before their work shift ended.

The night-shift lead operator in the spray dryer area arrived at the plant at 6:30 pm. The second spray dryer operator arrived at 7:00 pm.[3] Based on interviews, the lead operator slept from 7:00 pm until approximately 10:00 pm,[4] at which time the two operators reassembled the spray dryer system and began spray drying material fed from tank #1. They also began preparing the next batch of material in tank #2. To ensure a continuous flow of liquid to the spray dryer, the operators typically alternated the feed tanks, feeding out of one tank while the second one was prepared, then switching tanks as the in-service tank ran empty.

In preparing tank #2, the operators added the caramel liquid and the maltodextrin, and then began heating the mixture to 160°F.

Early in the shift, while the two operators were packaging the spray-dried product from tank #1 (in 50-pound plastic bags inside cardboard boxes), they placed incorrect labels on the shipping boxes. After discovering this error, they began to relabel the boxes while tank #2 was heating.

At approximately 2:00 am, the second operator observed caramel color running out of the agitator shaft seal at the top of tank #2 and down the sides; he called the lead operator over from the packaging area. As they were discussing the situation, one of the tank insulation retaining bands snapped. The lead operator asked the second operator to get the night-shift maintenance mechanic and then moved to the southwest side of tank #2, where the temperature gauge was located.

> *In preparing tank #2, the operators added the caramel liquid and the maltodextrin, and then began heating the mixture to 160°F. [At the same time, they were relabeling boxes.]*

> *. . . The second operator observed caramel color running out of the agitator shaft seal at the top of tank #2 and down the sides . . .*

> *The lead operator . . . moved to the southwest side of tank #2, where the temperature gauge was located. As the second operator left the spray dryer area to locate the maintenance mechanic, tank #2 exploded.*

---

[3]A third operator and a maintenance mechanic were onsite in other areas of the plant, and a fifth employee was working in the quality control laboratory.

[4]CSB includes this information for completeness of the investigative record. It is not believed that this factor was causally related to the incident.

As the second operator left the spray dryer area to locate the maintenance mechanic, tank #2 exploded. The lead operator's death was caused by massive trauma.

The western end of the DDW facility was extensively damaged. The five-story-tall spray dryer was toppled, and debris was scattered up to 150 yards from the source of the explosion.

The top head of the feed tank separated at the weld seam and was propelled approximately 100 yards to the west, landing on the CSX rail line on the north side of the facility. The shell split open in a roughly vertical line. It appears that it was propelled off its foundation and struck the 12,000-gallon aqua ammonia storage tank, located 15 feet to the west (Figure 3); and then ricocheted approximately 20 feet to the northeast, hitting the bottom of the spray dryer structure and toppling it.

The aqua ammonia storage tank was knocked off its foundation and piping was ripped loose, which resulted in the 26,000-pound aqua ammonia leak. An ammonia vapor cloud traveled southwest from the storage tank, toward neighboring homes.

The second operator and two other employees, standing two rooms away from the source of the explosion, were unable to return to the area due to debris, the sparking of electrical

Figure 3. Aqua ammonia storage tank
prior to removal from diked area.

connections, steam leaks, and the strong smell of natural gas from a broken fuel line. They called the Louisville 9-1-1 center to report the incident and immediately proceeded to isolate and shut down the area. The plant's automatic alarm system had already notified the DDW alarm service, which contacted the Louisville Fire Department.

The employees turned off the steam, shut down the plant boilers, and isolated the area before leaving, at which time the Louisville Fire and Police Departments had arrived on scene. Automatic valves on the natural gas system worked as intended, and there was no fire as a result of the explosion.

During the incident, the Louisville/Jefferson County EMA and the Metro Louisville Health Department obtained maximum ammonia readings of 50 parts per million (ppm) at the DDW fenceline and 35 ppm on Payne Street.[5] The Fire Department evacuated two blocks of Payne Street closest to the facility. Twenty-six residents were moved into buses at either end of Payne Street, but they did not leave the area. The Fire Department, emergency radio, and news media notified approximately 1,500 residents within 0.5 mile of DDW to shelter-in-place. No injuries were reported in the area of the ammonia release (Figure 4).

The Occupational Safety and Health Administration (OSHA) workplace exposure limit for ammonia is 50 ppm for an 8-hour workday.[6] The National Institute for Occupational Safety and Health has established a concentration of 300 ppm as "immediately dangerous to life and health" (IDLH; NIOSH, 1997).[7]

Automatic valves on the natural gas system worked as intended, and there was no fire as a result of the explosion.

. . . The Louisville/Jefferson County EMA and the Metro Louisville Health Department obtained maximum ammonia readings of 50 parts per million . . .

Twenty-six residents were moved into buses at either end of Payne Street . . .

The Fire Department, emergency radio, and news media notified approximately 1,500 residents within 0.5 mile of DDW to shelter-in-place.

---

[5] Some people may detect the odor of ammonia at concentrations as low as 1 ppm; others will not smell it until the concentration reaches 20 to 30 ppm. Levels of 25 to 50 ppm are irritating to the eyes, nose, throat, and lungs, but have no severe or irreversible health effects (see Section 4.5).

[6] OSHA Permissible Exposure Limit (PEL) for General Industry, 29 CFR 1910.1000, Toxic and Hazardous Substances, Table Z-1, Limits for Air Contaminants.

[7] NIOSH defines IDLH as a maximum 30-minute exposure level that allows a worker to escape without suffering loss of life or irreversible health effects. IDLH atmospheres can be entered only by persons wearing highly reliable breathing apparatus.

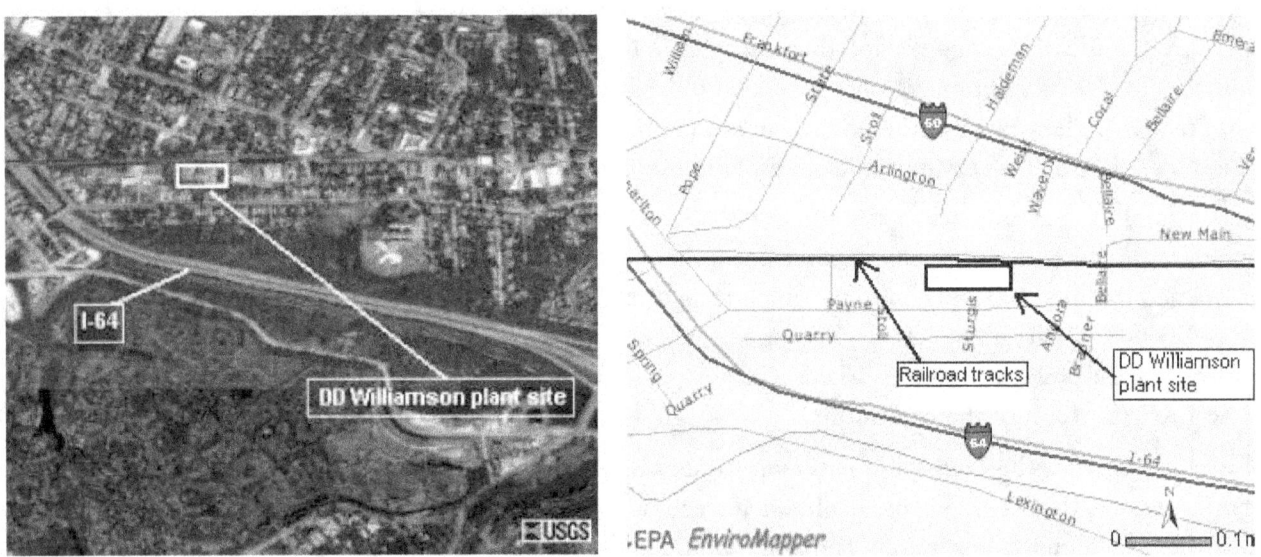

Figure 4. DDW aerial photograph and location map.

Because ammonia concentrations of 70 to 100 ppm were obtained in the immediate vicinity of the leak, the Fire Department hazardous materials unit personnel wore self-contained breathing apparatus and fully encapsulated suits. They made two entries into the blast area to search for the missing employee, to locate the source of the aqua ammonia leak, and to conduct air monitoring. At 7:00 am, a third entry was made with plant employees, who assisted in securing the leak. Residents were allowed to return to their homes at 9:00 am.

The explosive failure of feed tank #2 caused the fatality and damages at the DDW site. Sections 3.1 and 3.2 describe the effects of the explosion and other findings related to the causes of the incident.

3.1 Explosion Damage

3.1.1 Feed Tank #2

Feed tank #2 separated into three large pieces:

- The top head separated at the weld seam and flew approximately 100 yards to the west, landing on the CSX rail line on the north side of the facility (Figure 5).

Figure 5. Feed tank #2, top head.

- The shell split open in a roughly vertical line. It appears that it was propelled off its foundation and struck the aqua ammonia storage tank, located 15 feet to the west, and then ricocheted 20 feet to the northeast, hitting the bottom of the spray dryer structure and toppling it (Figure 6).

Figure 6. Feed tank #2 shell, after recovery.

Figure 7. Steam coil ejected from feed tank #2 (photographed in relocated position).

The valve and pipe were plugged with a hard, sticky black material—typical of overcooked caramel color liquid.

■ The bottom head was found directly beneath the tank shell, under the spray dryer structure.

The internal steam coil from tank #2 (Figure 7) was found approximately 30 feet to the south of the tank's original location. As the feed tank came apart, the coil was ejected and broke apart transversely. The coil retained its round configuration, indicating that the tank did not fail because of an internal deflagration or detonation, which would be expected to deform the coils—but because of pressure exerted somewhat evenly around the circumference of the vessel. CSB tested the coil to determine if a steam leak could have been a causal factor in the incident but was unable to determine whether the coil broke prior to, or as a result of, the explosion. No leaks were found in the intact portions of the coil.

The 1-inch vent valve and a portion of the vent pipe were recovered in a parking lot, approximately 250 feet west of the tank's original location. The valve and pipe were plugged with a hard, sticky black material—typical of overcooked caramel color liquid (Figures 8 and 9). As observed by CSB, the valve appeared to be approximately one-quarter open; however, due to the effects of the explosion, CSB was unable to ascertain the valve position prior to the event.

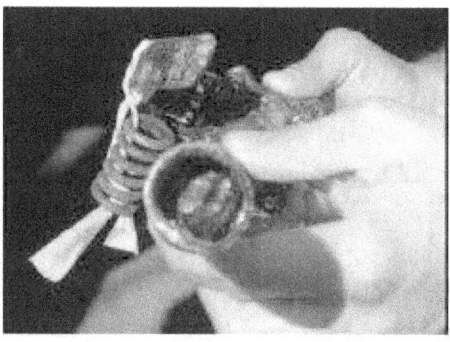

Figure 8. Plugged 1-inch vent pipe.

Figure 9. Closeup of vent pipe pluggage.

Other parts of feed tank #2, including the agitator shaft and agitator motor, were found in the general area of the top head—100 yards west of the tank location. The 100-pound motor flew 150 yards to the northwest, struck a sidewalk, and came to rest on the walkway leading to a house on Stoll Avenue.

3.1.2   Feed Tank #1

Feed tank #1 was propelled to the south and landed on its side, approximately 150 feet from its original location (Figure 10).

Feed tank #1

Figure 10. Feed tank #1

3.1.3   Aqua Ammonia Tank

The force of the explosion and impact with at least a portion of feed tank #2 pushed the 12,000-gallon horizontal aqua ammonia storage tank off its foundation saddles and approximately 10 feet to the west. This movement ruptured a line underneath the tank. The open valve on this line, located at the tank, was intact; however, it was buried in debris and caramel liquid.

The tank contained approximately 30,000 pounds (4,800 gallons) of aqua ammonia at the time of the incident. A vacuum truck recovered almost 4,000 pounds of aqua ammonia from the tank following the incident, indicating the loss of 26,000 pounds (equivalent to approximately 7,500 pounds of pure ammonia).

The leak rate over 5 hours was estimated at 5,000 pounds (800 gallons) per hour.

Because of the debris and ammonia vapors, emergency response and DDW personnel made three entries into the area before they were able to locate and secure the leak.

The leak rate over 5 hours was estimated at 5,000 pounds (800 gallons) per hour.

3.2   Other Effects of Explosion

Other effects of the explosion included the following:

- The spray dryer area at the west end of the DDW site was totally destroyed (Figure 11).

- A concrete block wall to the east of the spray dryer area collapsed.

- A 6-inch gas line ruptured; however, automatic valves prevented release of the natural gas.

The spray dryer area at the west end of the DDW site was totally destroyed.

Figure 11. Collapsed spray dryer structure.

4.0 Analysis of Incident

In analyzing the causes of this incident, CSB focused on the following issues:

- Overpressurization and lack of means to relieve pressure from the feed tanks.

- Lack of a system to identify safety hazards of the feed tanks and implement engineering or administrative controls.

4.1 Feed Tank Overpressure and Failure

Feed tank #2 most likely failed as a result of:

- Overheating of the caramel liquid, which generated pressure.

- Plugging of the vessel vent valve.

The tank had no overpressure protection.

Feed tank #2 most likely failed as a result of overheating of the caramel liquid, which generated pressure; [and] plugging of the vessel vent valve.

4.1.1 Incident Causation Scenario

Interviews with the surviving operator, other operators, and staff—and examination of physical evidence—led CSB to the following scenario for the overpressure event:

- The operators filled feed tank #2 with caramel color liquid, maltodextrin, and water.

- The operators began to heat the mixture; at the same time, they were relabeling the previously packaged product. The operators did not notice that the temperature of feed tank #2 had risen above the specified 160°F.

The operators did not notice that the temperature of feed tank #2 had risen above the specified 160°F.

Based on interview statements, CSB concluded that the operators did not adequately monitor the heating process and allowed the feed tank to overheat because they were preoccupied with the relabeling. There were no temperature alarms to warn of overheating and no temperature interlocks to automatically shut down the steam addition.

There were no temperature alarms to warn of overheating and no temperature interlocks to automatically shut down the steam addition.

The operators observed caramel liquid leaking from the agitator shaft seal at the top of the feed tank . . .

A tank insulation-retaining band snapped, indicating that the tank shell most likely expanded in response to increased pressure.

The 1-inch valve on the vent line was most likely closed as the caramel liquid heated . . . Evidence indicates that this quarter-turn ball valve and vent line—the only vent on the vessel—was plugged.

- It is possible that while heating up the batch, the operators also put air pressure on the feed tank to provide sufficient force to move the high-viscosity material to the spray dryer feed pump.[8] A regulator allowed approximately 22-psig air to pressurize the headspace of the feed tanks.

  Some operators applied air pressure while the feed tanks were heating; others added air pressure only when the material was at 160°F and ready to be transferred to the spray dryer. In either case, it was necessary to close the 1-inch vent valve to add air pressure.

- The operators observed caramel liquid leaking from the agitator shaft seal at the top of the feed tank, which indicated excess temperature and pressure on the tank. It is likely that the caramel liquid also flowed into the 1-inch vent line, filling and plugging it.

- A tank insulation-retaining band snapped, indicating that the tank shell most likely expanded in response to increased pressure.

- The 1-inch valve on the vent line was most likely closed as the caramel liquid heated. As the mixture overheated, expanding and emitting steam and vapor, material filled and plugged the vent line, blocking pressure relief. Evidence indicates that this quarter-turn ball valve and vent line—the only vent on the vessel—was plugged (Figures 8 and 9). The lead operator most likely opened the vent line valve but to no effect.

- The vessel failed catastrophically because it had no capability to release excess pressure.

CSB calculated a failure pressure of approximately 180 psi for a new vessel built to the specifications of feed tank #2. The Kentucky Boiler Inspection Section also estimated 180 psi. Because it is improbable that the pressure in the vessel exceeded the 130-psi steam used in the facility, the more likely cause of failure is a weakened feed tank. The tank had been deformed twice

---

[8]Because of the extent of damage, CSB was unable to determine the position of the compressed air valves.

due to misapplication of vacuum (though not while in Louisville), and the repairs were not inspected or certified to meet ASME Code requirements.

4.1.2 Alternative Incident Causation Scenarios

CSB considered and rejected a number of other potential failure scenarios because of the lack of sufficient supporting evidence:

- **Failure of the steam coil inside feed tank #2:** A failure of the steam coil could have generated sufficient pressure—from the steam (130 psi) and the vaporization of water—to cause the vessel explosion. Although the coil was torn apart, CSB could not determine if this failure was pre- or post-incident.

  The second operator, however, observed only liquid coming from the top of the feed tank prior to the explosion—not vapor or steam. It is likely that a major coil failure would have released steam through the agitator seal. The feed tank drawings noted that the steam coil was hydrostatically tested at 50 psi—which is much less than the 130-psi working pressure.

- **Excess air pressure due to failure of the feed tank air regulator:** Air from the plant air system, which is run at 125 psi, is added to the feed tanks to aid in pressurizing the mixture through the spray dryer feed pumps. This pressure level could have resulted in a catastrophic tank rupture if the regulator that controls airflow to the feed tank failed open.

  However, physical and eyewitness evidence indicates that heating was the key event. The stem of the heavily damaged regulator recovered from the scene was positioned very close to the valve seat, indicating that the regulator was likely functioning properly to control pressure. There is no connection between regulator failure and overheating. The extent of damage to the regulator precluded CSB from determining if the regulator failed open.

The second operator . . . observed only liquid coming from the top of the feed tank prior to the explosion— not vapor or steam. It is likely that a major coil failure would have released steam through the agitator seal.

The stem of the heavily damaged regulator recovered from the scene was positioned very close to the valve seat, indicating that the regulator was likely functioning properly to control pressure.

- **Chemical reaction due to contamination or product mixup:** The product being spray dried at the time of the incident is the only product in the DDW line that uses maltodextrin as the carrying agent. All other spray-dried products use lime. (Caramel color liquid reacts with lime, resulting in a temperature increase.)

Based on examination of the scene and chemical testing of substances at the scene, it was determined that the proper carrying agent—maltodextrin—had been added to the caramel liquid. No attempt was made to determine the temperature rise that would have occurred if lime had been added to the product instead of maltodextrin.

- **Return pressure from the spray dryer positive displacement feed pump:** The pump that moves material from the feed tanks to the spray dryer operates at approximately 4,000 psi. This very high pressures is necessary to achieve the degree of atomization required to produce the properly sized dried caramel color powder. If inadvertently returned to the spray dryer feed tank, this pressure would have been more than sufficient to cause vessel failure.

Although the feed pump piping was too badly damaged to allow for reconstruction, interviews with operators and management indicated that the piping system had no temporary connections. There was no way for pressure from the feed pump to return to the feed tank.

. . . The piping system had no temporary connections. There was no way for pressure from the feed pump to return to the feed tank.

Fabrication drawings indicate that the two feed tanks were designed for working pressures of 40 psi for tank #2 and 25 psi for tank #1. Although the tanks were operated as pressure vessels, there is no evidence that either tank was designed, fabricated, repaired, or tested in accordance with the ASME Code—which would have included certification by an authorized inspector. The certification process requires a visual inspection, review of fabrication details, and review of test results to ensure the integrity of the vessel at the rated pressure.

Certified vessels are registered with the National Board of Boiler and Pressure Vessel Inspectors[9] and are identified with an ASME stamp. At the time of the incident, the tanks were not equipped with pressure relief devices, such as relief valves or rupture disks—another ASME Code requirement. The Commonwealth of Kentucky requires vessel certification and the use of properly sized pressure relief devices.

Although the tanks were operated as pressure vessels, there is no evidence that either tank was designed, fabricated, repaired, or tested in accordance with the ASME Code . . .

4.2.1 Consensus Code Requirements

ASME first formulated rules for the construction of steam boilers and pressure vessels in 1911. The ASME Boiler and Pressure Vessel Code "establishes rules of safety governing the design, fabrication, and inspection of boilers and pressure vessels . . ." (ASME, 2001; p. 2)

The ASME Code, Section VIII (Rules for Construction of Pressure Vessels), requires that:

> . . . All vessels (having an internal operating pressure exceeding 15 psi) shall be provided with pressure relief devices . . . It is the responsibility of the user to ensure that the required pressure relief devices are properly installed prior to initial operation. (ASME, 2001; p. 93)

At the time of the incident, the tanks were not equipped with pressure relief devices, such as relief valves or rupture disks—another ASME Code requirement.

---

[9]The National Board of Boiler and Pressure Vessel Inspectors, created in 1919, oversees adherence to boiler and pressure vessel construction and repair codes. Among its functions, the Board commissions vessel inspectors and maintains records of all Board-registered boilers and pressure vessels.

4.2.2 Kentucky Pressure Vessel Regulations and DDW Compliance

The Commonwealth of Kentucky is among the 40 states that have adopted the ASME Code. It serves as the basis for the Kentucky Boiler and Pressure Vessel Safety Act (of 1962), which requires that:

> . . . Each . . . pressure vessel used or proposed to be used within this state . . . shall be thoroughly inspected as to their construction, installation and condition as follows: Pressure vessels shall be inspected at time of installation . . .[10]

Kentucky's adherence to the ASME Code for pressure vessels dates to 1980; for boilers, to 1964. The Kentucky Administrative Regulations (KAR), with detailed rules for boilers and pressure vessels, were promulgated under the Boiler and Pressure Vessel Safety Act. Both KAR and the Act define pressure vessels as operating at 15 psi or greater, in accordance with the ASME Code.

The Boiler Inspection Section of the Office of the State Fire Marshal—which is part of the Office of Housing, Building, and Construction under the Department of Public Protection, Environment and Public Protection Cabinet—administers the boiler and pressure vessel rules.

Kentucky law requires that all pressure vessels be certified by an inspector, registered with the National Board, and registered with the State. In addition, for used vessels, such as the DDW feed tanks, KAR states:

> . . . Before a vessel is brought into Kentucky for use, it shall be inspected by a boiler inspector or a special boiler inspector and the data shall be filed by the owner or user of the boiler or pressure vessel with the Boiler Inspection Section for approval.[11]

---

[10]Commonwealth of Kentucky, Kentucky Revised Statutes, Title 19, Chapter 236, Boiler and Pressure Vessel Safety Act, 236.110(1) and (1)(c).

[11]Commonwealth of Kentucky, KAR, Title 815, 15:026, Section 4, Used Vessels (1).

As detailed in Section 4.3, DDW staff did not consider the feed tanks to be pressure vessels. As a result, DDW did not notify the State when the feed tanks were brought into Kentucky, nor did it identify the tanks as pressure vessels for insurance purposes. State officials explained that proper notification triggers an inspection. In this instance, State inspectors stated that they would have rejected the vessels for lack of National Board registration.

Insurance company inspections occurred regularly at DDW; however, they focused on the two packaged boiler units and the pressure vessels in which the caramel liquid is produced.

[Because] DDW staff did not consider the feed tanks to be pressure vessels, the State [was not notified] when [they] were brought into Kentucky . . .

4.2.3 Comparison of State Regulatory Requirements and Practices

CSB compared Kentucky pressure vessel requirements with those of six neighboring states.[12] In general, Kentucky regulations and practices are similar to—or exceed—those of the other states surveyed.

The state officials surveyed agreed that unregistered vessels—and the states' inability to know of their use—are an ongoing problem. In all states surveyed, the owners/operators of the vessels or the contractors installing them are responsible for so notifying the state. Other means by which unregistered vessels may be reported include calls from building permit officials and inspectors, plumbing inspectors, and fire departments conducting routine facility inspections, to name a few. Kentucky makes use of all these notification methods; however, State officials were not aware of the use of the feed tanks at DDW until the incident occurred.

. . . Proper notification triggers an inspection. In this instance, State inspectors stated that they would have rejected the vessels for lack of National Board registration.

---

[12]CSB conducted phone interviews with the chief boiler inspectors of Indiana, North Carolina, Ohio, Pennsylvania, Tennessee, and Virginia.

Because of an exemption in the Kentucky regulations, DDW was not required to reinspect the feed tanks. KAR currently establishes an inspection exemption for new vessels based on maximum allowable pressure . . .

Kentucky allows certified boiler inspectors employed by insurance companies to reinspect boilers and pressure vessels, but State inspectors conduct all initial inspections.

Without the exemption, a large number of vessels rated less than 200 psi would fall under the purview of the Boiler Inspection Section—including, for example, compressed air receivers at vehicle service stations and garages.

Because of an exemption in the Kentucky regulations, DDW was not required to reinspect the feed tanks. KAR currently establishes an inspection exemption for new vessels based on *maximum allowable pressure*, stating under "Pressure Vessel Inspections" that:

> The following vessels shall be inspected upon installation and reinspected every three (3) years: Pressure vessels exceeding 200 psi maximum allowable pressure.[13]

This regulation exempts vessels rated less than 200 psi. However, Kentucky requires registration and an initial used vessel inspection before the vessel is brought into the State.

Kentucky allows certified boiler inspectors employed by insurance companies to *reinspect* boilers and pressure vessels, but State inspectors conduct all *initial* inspections. At one time, Kentucky allowed insurance companies to also inspect new installations; however, State officials eliminated this practice because of concerns about the lack of thoroughness of the inspections.

Kentucky boiler inspection officials explained that the exemption for lower pressure vessels is necessary based on budget and manpower restrictions (i.e., a current allotment of 10 inspectors). Without the exemption, a large number of vessels rated less than 200 psi would fall under the purview of the Boiler Inspection Section—including, for example, compressed air receivers at vehicle service stations and garages.

Several of the other states surveyed ensure that all pressure vessels receive adequate regulatory coverage—for example, by allowing insurance inspectors to inspect installations or by authorizing owners and users of pressure vessels to have inspections conducted by third-party or contract inspectors.[14]

---

[13]815 KAR 15:027, Section 1(7)(a).

[14]The Risk and Insurance Management Society, Inc. (RIMS), is an organization of 8,400 risk managers and insurance professionals. RIMS provides educational opportunities for its members in addition to publishing books and journals on safety and risk.

CSB is concerned that a large number of pressure vessels currently in service in Kentucky receive inadequate regulatory oversight. Although there is no causal relationship between this issue and the DDW incident, CSB wrote to the Commissioner of the Office of Housing, Building, and Construction requesting that the State look at other similar state programs for an efficient and economical means of eliminating this exemption.

4.3 Hazard Evaluation Systems and Technical Oversight

DDW did not have adequate hazard evaluation systems or procedures for the feed tank system. Furthermore, the company did not effectively use its consultants and contractors to evaluate and respond to the risks associated with the feed tanks.

As determined through interviews, DDW staff did not consider the two feed tanks to be pressure vessels—even though vessel drawings identified them as such, and approximately 20 to 25 psi of air pressure was added to help push each batch of caramel liquid to the spray dryer.

As a food producer, DDW is required to abide by regulations of the U.S. Food and Drug Administration (FDA). The FDA current Good Manufacturing Practice (cGMP) standards address issues such as cleanliness, quality control, and product safety. However, the standards do not address worker or manufacturing safety.

DDW did not have adequate hazard evaluation systems or procedures for the feed tank system.

Information and good practices on hazards and their prevention are widely available. The National Safety Council (NSC) *Accident Prevention Manual for Industrial Operations* notes:

> . . . Because pressure vessels are used to process such a great variety of materials, equip each vessel with safety devices designed for the type of vessel and for the work it is to do . . . The vessel should be provided with safety devices that will adequately protect it against overpressure, chemical reaction, or other abnormal conditions. (NSC, 1997; p. 492)

NSC also delineates a system for loss control, which is defined as:

> . . . The function directed toward recognizing, evaluating, and eliminating, or at least controlling, the destructive effects of occupational hazards . . . The primary function of a loss control system is to locate, assess, and set effective preventive and corrective measures for those elements detrimental to operational efficiency and effectiveness. (NSC, 1997; p. 76)

DDW should have used this type of safety information in developing systems for analysis of the feed tanks.

An engineering review of scenarios that could lead to exceedances of maximum vessel pressure is essential to determine overpressure protection requirements and to size protection devices. For vessels such as the feed tanks, a review would likely have identified the following possible events:

An engineering review of scenarios that could lead to exceedances of maximum vessel pressure . . . would likely have identified the following possible events:

- *Displacement of air.*
- *Failure of air regulator.*
- *Failure of steam coils.*
- *A reaction, for example, due to inadvertent mixing of incompatible materials.*
- *Overheating if steam is left in the coils too long.*

- Displacement of air as liquid product enters the tank.

- Failure of air regulator. (The plant air pressure was 125 psi, greater than the maximum allowable pressure of the feed tanks.)

- Failure of steam coils, releasing large amounts of steam into the tank. (The plant steam pressure was 130 psi, also greater than the maximum allowable pressure of the feed tanks.)

- A reaction, for example, due to inadvertent mixing of incompatible materials, such as lime and liquid caramel coloring.

- Overheating of the contents of the tank if steam is left in the coils too long.

There is no evidence that DDW conducted engineering reviews when the feed tanks were installed or modified. It is likely that such reviews would have identified the need for a properly sized relief valve to protect against the worst case overpressurization scenario.

It is likely that such [a] review would have identified the need for a properly sized relief valve to protect against the worst case overpressurization scenario.

Other instances of lack of overpressure protection were identified following the April 11 incident:

- Although the feed tank steam coils were designed with a test pressure of 50 psi, they were exposed to the full plant steam pressure of 130 psi.

  - The steam pressure should have been regulated to a level below the maximum coil design pressure.

  - The coils should have been protected from failure of the steam regulators.

- Insurance inspectors observed that the plant air compressor surge tank did not have overpressure protection. When DDW corrected this oversight, the set pressure specified for the installed relief valve was *at* or slightly *below* the discharge pressure of the air compressor. This set up a potentially hazardous situation where the relief valve, whose discharge was not vented to a safe location, could open at any time. State boiler inspectors observed this hazard during a review of the installation and pointed it out to DDW for immediate correction.

Despite the presence of experienced personnel, the need for overpressure protection and additional engineering controls for the feed tanks was not identified (Section 4.4).

The absence of adequate hazard evaluation systems as a component of basic plant engineering practices has been a causal factor in a number of incidents at small companies, including Catalyst Systems and Third Coast Industries (USCSB, 2003a; 2003b).

DDW used contract engineering services, when necessary, for environmental permitting, installation and subsequent modification of the spray dryer system, and development of the Risk Management Program (RMP) package for the aqua ammonia tank (Section 4.5). DDW also relied on insurance audits as a check on its engineering practices. As noted earlier, these inspections and services did not note the use of the feed tanks as pressure vessels.

Although the feed tank steam coils were designed with a test pressure of 50 psi, they were exposed to the full plant steam pressure of 130 psi.

Despite the presence of experienced personnel, the need for overpressure protection and additional engineering controls for the feed tanks was not identified.

4.4 Engineering and Administrative Controls

"Layers of protection" is a safety design concept used in engineering hazardous systems. *Guidelines for Engineering Design for Process Safety,* published by the Center for Chemical Process Safety (CCPS) of the American Institute of Chemical Engineers (AIChE), explains the concept for designing and operating process equipment:

> These layers of protection start with the basic process design and include control systems, alarms and interlocks, safety shutdown systems, protective systems and response plans . . . (CCPS, 1993; p. 9)

The spray dryer feed tanks lacked sufficient layers of protection to protect DDW workers from the hazards of the operation:

Except for the use of weigh cells to control and monitor tank level, safe operation of the spray dryer feed tanks was dependent on the attentiveness and experience of each operator . . .

- Except for the use of weigh cells to control and monitor tank level, safe operation of the spray dryer feed tanks was dependent on the attentiveness and experience of each operator to ensure that the system stayed within temperature and pressure operating parameters.

- The operators had little guidance on how to control the equipment or on what actions to take in the event of unusual occurrences.

There were no alarms in the feed tank system to alert operators of abnormal conditions . . .

- There were no alarms in the feed tank system to alert operators of abnormal conditions—which increased the likelihood that they would miss the warning signs of tank failure.

- There were no interlocks to automatically shut down the feed tank portion of the spray dryer system if safe operating limits were exceeded.

There were no overpressure protection devices in the form of pressure relief valves.

- There were no overpressure protection devices in the form of pressure relief valves.

4.4.1 Pressure Control

Operators manually added 20 to 25 psi of air pressure to each batch in the feed tanks to provide sufficient pressure to operate the spray dryer feed pumps. To pressurize the tanks, operators closed the 1-inch vent valve and opened a valve on the air line. An air regulator reduced air from the plant air compressor (at 125 psi) to 25 psi. The vent valve was intended to be kept open at all times, except when pressure was added to a feed tank for pumping into the spray dryer.

The vent valve was intended to be kept open at all times, except when pressure was added to a feed tank for pumping into the spray dryer.

4.4.2 Temperature Control

The caramel color liquid was heated to approximately 160°F to reduce its viscosity and to improve flowability to the spray dryer feed pumps and through the atomizer nozzles. To increase the temperature, operators manually opened valves to allow 130-psig steam (350°F) into the feed tank internal coils. As heat was transferred to the caramel color liquid, the steam condensed and was removed through steam traps on the coil outlets.

The operators used a gauge on the side of the feed tanks to monitor the temperature of the caramel liquid. There were no alarms to alert the operators if temperatures exceeded prescribed limits and no automatic shutdown mechanisms. For example, an automatic shutdown system would close valves in the steam supply to vessel heating coils when a prescribed high temperature trip point was reached.

The operators used a gauge on the side of the feed tanks to monitor the temperature of the caramel liquid. There were no alarms . . . and no automatic shutdown mechanisms.

4.4.3 Operating Procedures and Training

DDW operators used batch sheets to guide them through the production processes. A typical batch sheet for the spray dryer area required the operator to list the quantities of various raw materials used in the batch. At specific times during the drying process, determined by the number of boxes that were packaged, the operators would enter information about drying conditions and take samples for quality determination in the DDW laboratory. The batch sheets contained no safety information, warnings, or guidance concerning operation of the equipment or steps to take in unusual situations.

Good written procedures—such as those meeting the requirements of the OSHA Process Safety Management (PSM) Standard or the U.S. Environmental Protection Agency (EPA) RMP regulation—require information on:

- Consequences of deviation from operating limits and corrective steps.

- Safety and health.

- Safety systems and their functions.

The inclusion of this type of information on the batch sheets would have provided DDW operators with reminders of the hazards of the operation and necessary precautions.

Interviews with operators indicated that the feed tanks heated very rapidly. It typically took only 20 to 30 minutes to heat a batch to the required temperature. Most of the operators interviewed noted that there were times when they forgot to closely monitor the temperature and it exceeded 200°F. On these occasions, the 1-inch vent valve remained open and a large amount of steam was expelled, but there were no other deleterious effects. Management was aware of these temperature excursions, but took no actions to modify operating procedures or to install automatic controls or alarms.

None of the operating or maintenance employees could recall past instances of the 1-inch vent valve being plugged. However, personnel noted that it took 15 to 20 minutes of very loud venting to release pressure through the line after the vessel was emptied of feed, indicating that pressure built up in the tank during each batch. As shown in Figures 7 and 8, the vent line and valve recovered after the incident were plugged with hardened caramel color liquid.

The typical order of operations was to heat the caramel liquid to the specified temperature and then add air pressure. The batch could then be held until the other feed tank was emptying out, and the feed flow switched to the ready tank. However, operators also stated that it was possible to combine the two operations, adding air pressure while the temperature was being raised.

DDW written procedures did not explain the risks of overheating the feed tanks when the vent valves were closed. Operators relied on their experience to judge the length of time necessary to heat a feed tank; practices differed slightly among operators.

At DDW, a new operator was paired with an experienced operator to learn the required job assignments. Safety meetings were held to explain general safety concepts, such as fire safety, hazard communication, and emergency plans. On the night of the incident, the lead operator—with 5 years experience—was teamed with a new operator hired 3 months earlier.

DDW written procedures did not explain the risks of overheating the feed tanks when the vent valves were closed. Operators relied on their experience to judge the length of time necessary to heat a feed tank . . .

4.5 Risk Management Program for Aqua Ammonia and Emergency Response

As required, DDW had submitted a Risk Management Plan to EPA for the storage and use of aqua ammonia. The EPA RMP is a product of the Clean Air Act Amendments of 1990. In many ways, RMP mirrors the OSHA PSM Standard. However, RMP focuses on protecting the public and the environment from offsite consequences, while the PSM Standard addresses catastrophic events that could have onsite consequences for workers.

The RMP threshold quantity for ammonia in concentrations of 20 percent or greater is 20,000 pounds. The aqua ammonia storage tank at DDW had a capacity of 88,000 pounds.

Although DDW exceeded the RMP threshold quantity for aqua ammonia, it did not handle ammonia at a high enough concentration to be covered by the OSHA PSM Standard, which applies only to solutions that contain greater than 44 percent ammonia.

Although DDW exceeded the RMP threshold quantity for aqua ammonia, it did not handle ammonia at a high enough concentration to be covered by the OSHA PSM Standard, which applies only to solutions that contain greater than 44 percent ammonia.

As described by EPA, there is a significant difference between the emissions from a release of aqua ammonia versus anhydrous ammonia:

> The principal difference between aqueous [aqua] ammonia and anhydrous ammonia, in the context of atmospheric dispersion modeling, is that the former evaporates relatively slowly from a pool, entirely as a vapor, whereas the latter consists of a mixture of vapor and liquid droplets that is initially denser than air. By contrast, the vapor from a pool of aqueous ammonia is neutrally buoyant, or even marginally lighter than air. (USEPA, 1999; pp. 3-17)

As a result, releases of aqua ammonia may have lesser consequences than anhydrous ammonia; much less ammonia vapor is produced, and it tends to disperse more quickly because it is lighter than air. This phenomenon was observed during the DDW incident.

The highest concentrations of ammonia in air—other than in the immediate area of the aqua ammonia tank—were measured by the Louisville/Jefferson County EMA at the DDW fenceline (50 ppm) and at Payne Street (35 ppm).

Because the ammonia leak occurred in the early morning and the explosion caused extensive damage, short-term community evacuation was a prudent step. In proximity to the leak—where concentrations reached IDLH levels—emergency responders wore personal protective equipment. At the facility fenceline and at Payne Street, ammonia concentrations were above the OSHA and NIOSH maximum exposure levels. However, these levels are specified for worker exposure and are not designed for the general public—which may include infants, the elderly, and those with compromised respiratory function.

. . . Releases of aqua ammonia may have lesser consequences than anhydrous ammonia; much less ammonia vapor is produced, and it tends to disperse more quickly because it is lighter than air. This phenomenon was observed during the DDW incident.

5.0   Root Causes

1. **D. D. Williamson did not have effective programs in place to determine if equipment and processes met basic process and plant engineering requirements.**

   - There was no program to evaluate necessary layers of protection on the spray dryer feed tanks. Likewise, there was no recognition of the need to provide process control and alarm instrumentation on the two feed tanks. Reliance on a single local temperature indicator that must be read by operators is insufficient. On the morning of the incident, the operators were unaware that the system had exceeded normal operating conditions.

   - The feed tanks were installed for use in the spray dryer process without a review of their design versus system requirements.

   - Safety valves on the spray dryer feed tanks had been removed to transport the tanks to Louisville and were never reinstalled. There was no evidence that DDW conducted an engineering evaluation to determine the hazards of this change.

2. **D. D. Williamson did not have adequate hazard analysis systems to identify feed tank hazards, nor did it effectively use contractors and consultants to evaluate and respond to associated risks.**

   - Neither DDW nor its contractors and consultants recognized the need for overpressure protection for the two feed tanks used in the spray dryer process.

   - DDW did not register the feed tanks as pressure vessels, as required by the Commonwealth of Kentucky.

3. D. D. Williamson did not have adequate operating procedures or adequate training programs to ensure that operators were aware of the risks of allowing the spray dryer feed tanks to overheat and knew how to respond appropriately.

- Operating procedures did not document:
  - Hazards of allowing the temperature of the feed tank to exceed normal operating conditions.
  - Hazards of heating a batch when the vent valve is closed.
  - Appropriate operator response to highly hazardous abnormal situations.
- Operators were not trained to keep the vent valve open until completion of the process of heating the feed tank batch.

6.0 Recommendations

1. Institute procedures to ensure that pressure vessels are designed, fabricated, and operated according to applicable codes and standards. (2003-11-I-KY-R1)

2. Audit all vessels at all D. D. Williamson facilities and ensure that they are (2003-11-I-KY-R2):

   - Equipped with adequate overpressure protection, as warranted.

   - Equipped with alarms or interlocks, as warranted.

3. Implement a program to review existing equipment when it is used for new purposes and when safety devices are removed or altered. (2003-11-I-KY-R3)

4. Implement a hazard evaluation procedure to determine the potential for catastrophic incidents and necessary safeguards. (2003-11-I-KY-R4)

5. Audit manual control of process conditions, such as temperature and pressure, and determine if safeguards are needed. (2003-11-I-KY-R5)

6. Upgrade written operating procedures and train operators on the revised procedures. (2003-11-I-KY-R6)

Communicate to the owners of pressure vessels, mechanical contractors, engineering consulting companies, and insurance companies doing business in Kentucky that used pressure vessels are not exempt from registration and initial inspection before being placed in service in Kentucky. (2003-11-I-KY-R7)

Mechanical Contractors Association of Kentucky	Communicate to your members that used pressure vessels are not exempt from registration and initial inspection before being placed in service in Kentucky. (2003-11-I-KY-R8)
Risk and Insurance Management Society (RIMS)	Communicate the findings of this report to your membership. (2003-11-I-KY-R9)
National Board of Boiler and Pressure Vessel Inspectors	Communicate the findings of this report to your membership. (2003-11-I-KY-R10)

By the

U.S. CHEMICAL SAFETY AND HAZARD INVESTIGATION BOARD

Carolyn W. Merritt
Chair

John S. Bresland
Member

Rixio E. Medina
Member

Gerald V. Poje, Ph.D.
Member

March 12, 2004

7.0 References

American Society of Mechanical Engineers (ASME), 2001. "Rules for Construction of Pressure Vessels, Part UG-125(a), General Requirements, Pressure Relief Devices," *ASME Boiler and Pressure Vessel Code*, Section VIII, Division 1.

Center for Chemical Process Safety (CCPS), 1993. *Guidelines for Engineering Design for Process Safety*, American Institute of Chemical Engineers (AIChE).

Kamuf, W., A. Nixon, and O. Parker, 2000. "Caramel Color," *Natural Food Colorants Science and Technology*, Chapter 12, G. J. Lauro and F. J. France, eds., Marcel Dekker, Inc.

National Institute for Occupational Safety and Health (NIOSH), 1997. *NIOSH Pocket Guide to Chemical Hazards*, DHHS Publication No. 97-140.

National Safety Council (NSC), 1997. *Accident Prevention Manual for Business and Industry*, 11th Edition.

U.S. Chemical Safety and Hazard Investigation Board (USCSB), 2003a. *Case Study, Fire and Explosion: Hazards of Benzoyl Peroxide, Catalyst Systems, Inc., Gnadenhutten, Ohio, January 2, 2003*, No. 2003-03-C-OH, October 2003.

U.S. Chemical Safety and Hazard Investigation Board (USCSB), 2003b. *Investigation Report, Petroleum Products Facility Incident, Third Coast Industries, Friendswood, Texas, May 1, 2002*, Report No. 2002-03-I-TX, March 2003.

U.S. Environmental Protection Agency (USEPA), 1999. *Technical Background Document for Offsite Consequence Analysis for Anhydrous Ammonia, Aqueous Ammonia, Chlorine, and Sulfur Dioxide*, Chemical Emergency Preparedness and Prevention Office, April 1999.

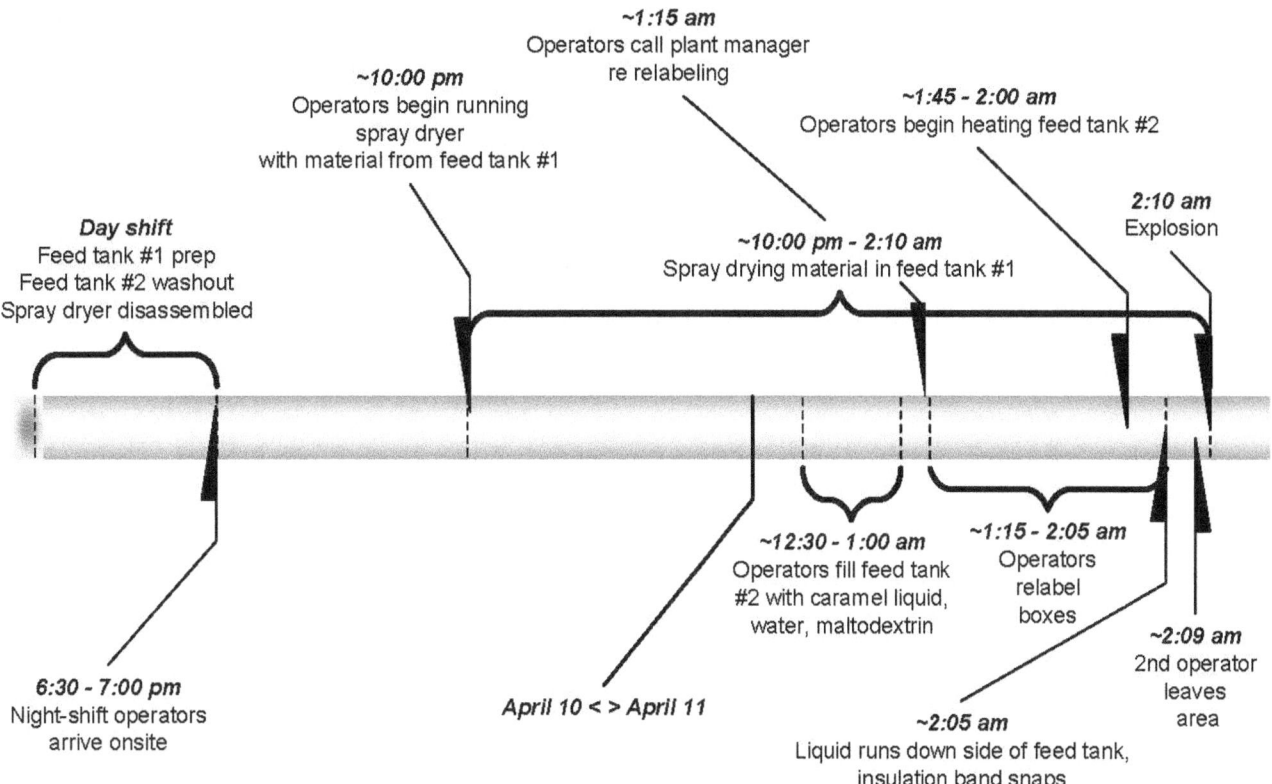

~1:15 am
Operators call plant manager
re relabeling

~10:00 pm
Operators begin running
spray dryer
with material from feed tank #1

~1:45 - 2:00 am
Operators begin heating feed tank #2

2:10 am
Explosion

Day shift
Feed tank #1 prep
Feed tank #2 washout
Spray dryer disassembled

~10:00 pm - 2:10 am
Spray drying material in feed tank #1

~12:30 - 1:00 am
Operators fill feed tank
#2 with caramel liquid,
water, maltodextrin

~1:15 - 2:05 am
Operators
relabel
boxes

~2:09 am
2nd operator
leaves
area

6:30 - 7:00 pm
Night-shift operators
arrive onsite

April 10 < > April 11

~2:05 am
Liquid runs down side of feed tank,
insulation band snaps

APPENDIX B: Logic Diagram

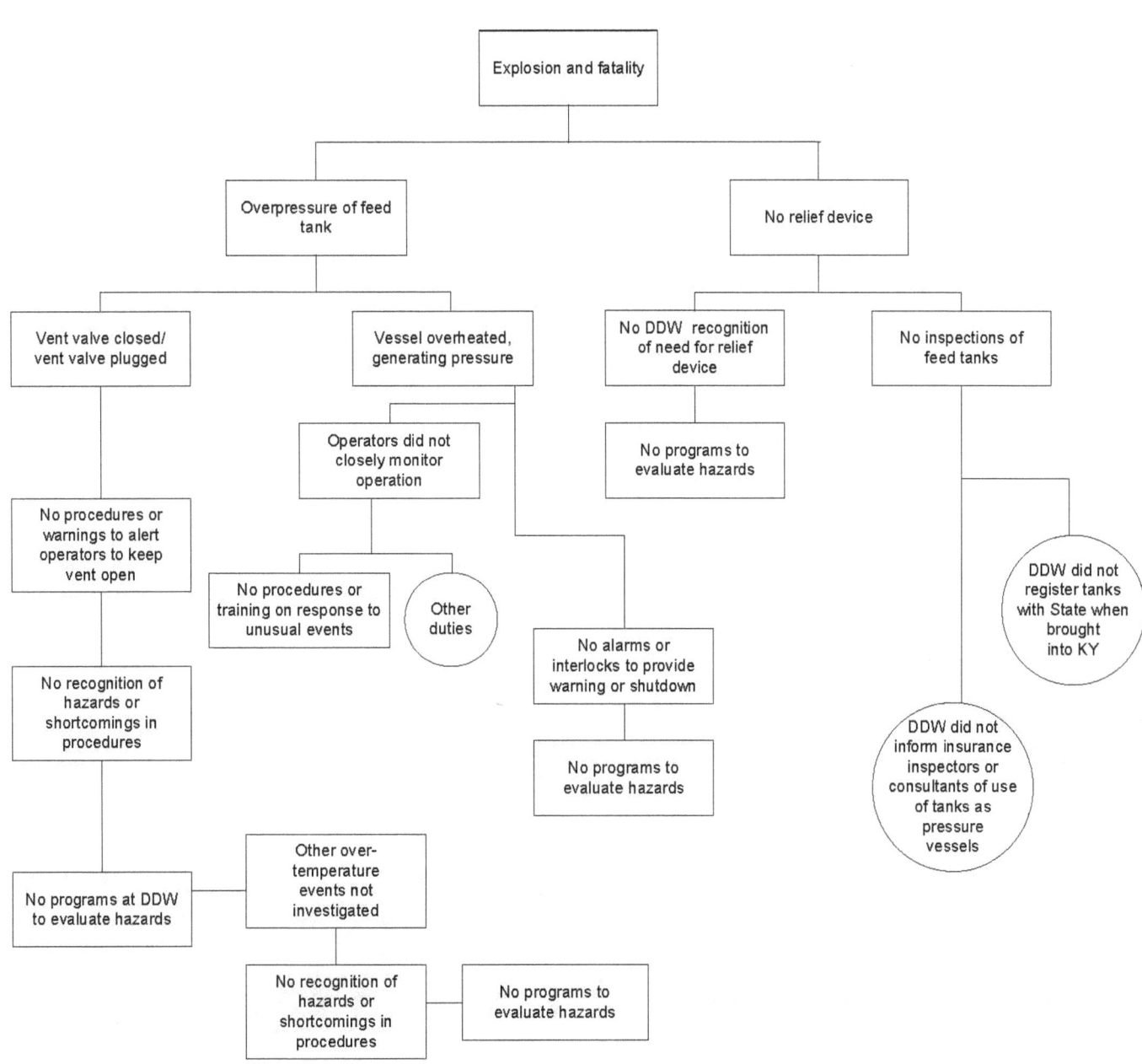

www.ingramcontent.com/pod-product-compliance
Lightning Source LLC
Chambersburg PA
CBHW081620170526
45166CB00009B/3042